Adultery Was Never God's Will
The Aftermath On The Family

By

Brenda Diann Johnson

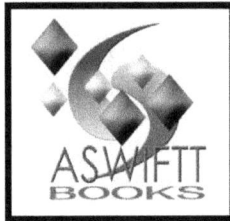

ASWIFTT ENTERPRISES, LLC
Duncanville, Texas 75138

Brenda Diann Johnson
E-mail: brendadiannjohnson@yahoo.com

Published by
ASWIFTT ENTERPRISES, LLC
Imprint: ASWIFTT BOOKS
P.O. Box 380669
Duncanville, Texas 75138-0669

ISBN: 978-0-9910816-5-3

Library of Congress Control Number: 2025948381

Printed in the United States of America

All scripture quotations are from the King James Version of the Bible unless otherwise noted.

Cover Design and Editing by Brenda Diann Johnson

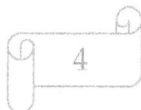

Dedications

I dedicate this book to couples who have mastered the art of being married according to God's Word, the Holy Scriptures.

I also dedicate this book to those who have provided an example for the rest of us who are still learning and striving to get it right in our own marriages.

Thank you for not giving up on each other while providing a light that leads marriages back to our Lord and Savior Jesus Christ.

Acknowledgments

I acknowledge an Almighty God who provided the blueprint for marriage in the Holy Scriptures. I also acknowledge it is God who places who He chooses to be apart of His Church that is His Bride.

Table of Contents

Introduction

Introduction

The narrative of David and Bathsheba stands as one of the most recognized and thought-provoking stories in the Bible. It illustrates how a solitary act of disobedience can disrupt not only an individual life but also a kingdom and potentially affect future generations. This account commences in 2 Samuel 11, where King David, once a humble shepherd and regarded as a man after God's own heart, makes a sequence of decisions that lead him away from righteousness and into wrongdoing. His choice to gaze upon, desire, and pursue Bathsheba would significantly change his life trajectory and legacy.

During an era when kings were expected to engage in battle, David opted to stay in Jerusalem. One evening, while walking on his rooftop, he noticed Bathsheba bathing. Rather than averting his eyes, he sought information about her and learned she was the wife of Uriah the Hittite, one of his loyal soldiers. Despite this knowledge, David summoned her and engaged in adultery. This single act triggered a cascade of deceit, murder, and anguish.

The transgression involving David and Bathsheba transcended mere lust; it involved coveting another's spouse, contravening God's commandments, and misusing authority. The narrative conveys that even those chosen by God are vulnerable to temptation and must face accountability for their actions. Each decision we make produces consequences that can extend well beyond ourselves.

In this book, we will delve into what transpired during this incident, how it unfolded, and the enduring repercussions of David's actions. We will uncover the lessons intended for us through this event—how obedience, humility, and repentance can pave the way for restoration.

As we move into Chapter I, our focus will be on examining in detail the events between David and Bathsheba—the nature of their encounter, the resulting betrayal, and the moral as well as spiritual implications that ensued.

What Happened?

Chapter I
What Happened?

The details of David and Bathsheba's infidelity is recounted in 2 Samuel 11:1–27. David's act of summoning Bathsheba violated a sacred boundary, leading to their adulterous encounter. Shortly thereafter, Bathsheba informed David of her pregnancy, which thrust him into a moral dilemma. Rather than confessing his wrongdoing to God, David attempted to conceal his sin, initiating a cascade of deceit and betrayal.

In an effort to cover up the situation, David summoned Uriah from the battlefield under the pretense of concern for the troops, hoping Uriah would return home and sleep with his wife, thereby attributing the pregnancy to him. However, Uriah demonstrated loyalty by refusing to indulge in personal comforts while his comrades were engaged in combat. Frustrated by Uriah's integrity, David sent him back to the front lines carrying a letter that effectively sealed his fate. This act of conspiracy and murder was not only a transgression against Uriah but also an affront to God Himself (2 Samuel 12:9).

David's act of adultery prompted further sins—deception, manipulation, and murder—illustrating how a single instance of disobedience can spiral into multiple transgressions. Upon learning of her husband's death, Bathsheba grieved deeply. After her period of mourning concluded, David married her and she bore him a son. Nevertheless, Scripture notes that "the thing that David had done displeased the Lord" (2 Samuel 11:27).

This episode in David's life exemplifies how even the most devout individuals can descend into moral failure when they deviate from divine commands. The roots of adultery do not lie merely in the physical act; they often begin with a glance, an unguarded thought, or unchecked desire devoid of reverence for God. David's actions were driven by covetousness and led him down a path of grave sin.

Scripture cautions us with the warning: "Be sure your sin will find you out" (Numbers 32:23). Ultimately, David's hidden transgressions would be brought to light by God through the prophet Nathan.

Reflection Questions:

1. What moral laws did David break in this story?

2. How did David's attempt to cover his sin make matters worse?

3. Why is coveting considered the root of David's downfall?

4. What can we learn about accountability from David's choices?

5. How can believers guard against the small compromises that lead to great sin?

For Further Study:

Exodus 20:14; Exodus 20:17; Proverbs 6:32; Proverbs 12:22; 2 Samuel 11:1–27; Psalm 51:1–4; Numbers 32:23; Matthew 5:28; James 1:14–15; Luke 12:2.

How Did It Happen?

Chapter II
How Did It Happen?

David's transgression did not happen abruptly; rather, it was the culmination of a slow build-up of temptation, desire, and unwise decisions. According to 2 Samuel 11:1, this incident took place during the season "when kings go off to war," yet David chose to remain behind. By shirking his responsibilities, he inadvertently invited temptation into his life. His inactivity provided a fertile ground for sin to flourish.

While strolling on his rooftop, David noticed Bathsheba bathing. Rather than diverting his gaze, he entertained the thought of her beauty. This lustfulness took hold in his heart and prompted him to inquire about her identity. Even after discovering that she was married, he permitted his emotions and authority to overshadow God's commandments. This constituted a blatant act of disobedience and an abuse of power. In his role as king, David exploited his position to seize what was not rightfully his.

Infidelity often begins with a glance that lingers too long or a thought that is nurtured instead of dismissed. David's initial lust devolved into deceit and manipulation as he schemed to conceal his wrongdoing. Once lust takes root, it gives rise to sin, which ultimately leads to death (James 1:15). David's betrayal extended beyond Uriah; it was also sin against God Himself (Psalm 51:4).

The ramifications are amplified when leaders misuse their power and resources. David's actions serve as a reminder that God demands integrity from those in influential positions. Deceit, secrecy, and falsehood can undermine the spiritual foundation of any individual or relationship.

David's experience illustrates the peril of indulging in temptation instead of fleeing from it. Allowing sin to take hold in our hearts can lead to deep-seated roots that result in destruction.

Reflection Questions:

1. What were David's first steps toward sin?

2. How does idleness open the door to temptation?

3. Why is abuse of power so dangerous?

4. What could David have done differently to avoid sin?

5. How does obedience protect us from destruction?

For Further Study:

2 Samuel 11:1–5; James 1:14–15; Proverbs 4:23; Matthew 5:28; Genesis 39:7–12; Galatians 5:19–21; 1 Corinthians 6:18; Psalm 101:3; 1 John 2:16; Romans 6:12.

The Consequences

Chapter III
The Consequences

David's wrongdoing with Bathsheba had severe repercussions, both in the short and long term. Following the birth of Bathsheba's child, God sent the prophet Nathan to admonish David (2 Samuel 12:1–14). Through a parable, Nathan unveiled David's transgressions, and although David expressed remorse, God's judgment was pronounced: "The sword shall never depart from your house" (2 Samuel 12:10). The child conceived through adultery ultimately died as a consequence of David's actions.

In the immediate aftermath, David faced profound loss, sorrow, and public disgrace. His authority diminished significantly, leading to chaos within his household. Over time, his family endured tragic outcomes. David's daughter Tamar was raped by her half-brother Amnon, which resulted in her brother Absalom avenging her by killing Amnon (2 Samuel 13). Subsequently, Absalom staged a rebellion against David with intentions to dethrone and kill him (2 Samuel 15).

The once-harmonious kingdom of David fell victim to internal conflict. Despite receiving forgiveness, he still had to face the repercussions of his sin. Spiritually, his lineage also suffered — Solomon, despite his wisdom, ultimately turned away from God to worship idols and engage with numerous wives (1 Kings 11:1–10).

Sin invariably leaves an imprint. While God forgives transgressions, the consequences of disobedience can persist for generations. The choices made by David impacted not only his life but also that of his descendants.

This chapter serves as a reminder that forgiveness does not eliminate consequences. The penalty for sin is death; however, God's grace provides redemption for those who genuinely repent from their hearts.

Reflection Questions:

1. What were the short-term and long-term consequences of David's sin?

2. How did Nathan's confrontation bring David to repentance?

3. Why does God sometimes allow consequences even after forgiveness?

4. How did David's sin affect his family and kingdom?

5. What lessons can we learn about accountability and repentance?

For Further Study:

2 Samuel 12:1–23; 2 Samuel 13:1–22; 2 Samuel 15:10–14; 1 Kings 11:1–10; Psalm 51:10–12; Proverbs 6:32–33; Galatians 6:7–8; Numbers 14:18; Hebrews 12:6; Romans 6:23.

A Teachable Lesson

Chapter IV
A Teachable Lesson

David's narrative serves as a compelling reminder that obedience holds greater value than sacrifice (1 Samuel 15:22). Despite his significant sins, David displayed sincere repentance upon being confronted. Psalm 51 captures his earnest plea: "Have mercy upon me, O God... create in me a clean heart, O God, and renew a right spirit within me." His humility and contrition mended his relationship with God.

Similarly, Bathsheba experienced restoration. Following the death of their first child, God granted her another son, Solomon, who would eventually become king. Even amid her sorrow, God transformed her grief into joy. This illustrates that even during times of judgment, God's mercy can lead to fresh beginnings.

The lesson to be learned from David's transgressions is that sin creates a divide between us and God; however, repentance can bridge that gap. God seeks obedience rather than mere external acts of sacrifice. Authentic repentance involves more than expressing regret; it requires turning away from sin and pursuing righteousness.

David's life also underscores the responsibility inherent in leadership. Those in positions of authority must govern with integrity and reverence for the Lord since their behavior sets an example for others.

When we stumble, restoration is possible; however, we should never assume grace is guaranteed. While God offers forgiveness, He also calls His people towards holiness and obedience.

Reflection Questions:

1. Why is obedience better than sacrifice?

2. How did David show true repentance?

3. How was Bathsheba restored after tragedy?

4. What role does humility play in restoration?

5. What does this story teach us about God's mercy?

For Further Study:

Psalm 51:1–17; 1 Samuel 15:22; 2 Samuel 12:24–25; 1 John 1:9; Isaiah 55:7; Luke 15:11–24; Proverbs 28:13; 2 Chronicles 7:14; Micah 7:18–19; Romans 8:1.

Other Cases Of Adultery

Chapter V
Other Cases Of Adultery

Adultery is not limited to the account of David and Bathsheba. It is a recurring theme throughout Scripture. God cautions His followers about its consequences, illustrating how infidelity can devastate relationships, families, and entire nations. In Genesis 39, the story of Joseph and Potiphar's wife highlights this point. Unlike David, who succumbed to temptation, Joseph chose to flee, declaring, "How then can I do this great wickedness, and sin against God?" (Genesis 39:9). Although his commitment resulted in a temporary loss of freedom, it ultimately safeguarded his integrity and future.

The Bible explicitly categorizes adultery as a transgression that breaches the sacred bond between spouses. The commandment in Exodus 20:14 states, "Thou shalt not commit adultery." Jesus later elaborated on this in Matthew 5:27–28 by teaching that the roots of adultery lie in the heart when someone gazes upon another with lustful desire. Adultery not only violates marital vows but also corrupts the body, regarded as the temple of the Holy Spirit (1 Corinthians 6:18–20).

According to biblical teachings, a husband and wife are united for life. Romans 7:2–3 explains that "For the woman which hath a husband is bound by the law to her husband so long as he liveth." Marrying another while one's spouse is still alive constitutes adultery. Similarly, 1 Corinthians 7:10–11 advises that if a wife separates from her husband, she must either remain single or reconcile with him.

Divorce is permitted under specific circumstances. In Matthew 19:8–9, Jesus indicated that divorce was allowed due to people's hardened hearts; however, he emphasized that it was not part of God's original design. He stated that "Whosoever shall put away his wife, except it be for fornication, and shall marry another, committeth adultery." Thus, sexual immorality or unfaithfulness stands as the sole biblical justification for divorce. Even in such cases, forgiveness and reconciliation should be sought if both parties are willing to repent.

When separation takes place among believers, they are encouraged to conduct themselves peacefully and honorably. If there is an opportunity for reconciliation, they should strive for it; otherwise, they must remain faithful to God and uphold their purity. The sanctity of marriage symbolizes Christ's relationship with the Church—rooted in covenantal commitment, sacrifice, and love (Ephesians 5:22–33).

Reflection Questions:

1. What does the Bible teach about the permanence of marriage?

2. Why does Jesus consider lust to be adultery of the heart?

3. Under what condition does the Bible permit divorce?

4. What is God's plan for separated spouses?

5. How does marriage reflect Christ's relationship with the Church?

For Further Study:

Genesis 39:7–12; Exodus 20:14; Matthew 5:27–28; Matthew 19:3–9; Romans 7:2–3; 1 Corinthians 7:10–16; Ephesians 5:22–33; Hebrews 13:4; Malachi 2:13–16; Mark 10:2–12.

Conclusion

Conclusion

The story of David and Bathsheba illustrates the perils of unbridled desire and the significant repercussions of disobedience. It serves as a reminder that sin, regardless of how concealed, carries public ramifications. David's transgressions—stemming from his longing for another man's spouse—culminated in adultery, deceit, and even murder. The commandment "Thou shalt not covet" (Exodus 20:17) was violated long before he acted on his desires. His wrongdoing impacted not only himself but also Bathsheba, Uriah, his children, and the entire nation of Israel.

According to biblical principles, an ideal marriage is a lifelong commitment between one man and one woman united under God. Genesis 2:24 declares, "Therefore shall a man leave his father and mother, and shall cleave unto his wife: and they shall be one flesh." Marriage is intended by God to embody unity, faithfulness, and love—reflecting the same love Christ has for His Church. When spouses engage in obedience, respect, and mutual honor, their union glorifies God.

Our decisions carry implications that extend across generations. David's actions inflicted suffering on his descendants; similarly, our choices can either bless or curse the future generations. Exodus 34:7 cautions that the consequences of sin may affect up to three or four generations; however, God's mercy reaches thousands who adhere to His commands. This reality encourages us to lead righteous lives and instill obedience in our children.

When believers follow God's directives regarding purity, fidelity, and repentance, they are rewarded with His favor and peace. Adultery and infidelity erode trust; conversely, repentance coupled with obedience reinstates it. God calls us to lead holy lives that honor Him in our relationships and decisions.

In concluding this examination of David's experience, let us view it not merely as a tale of failure but as one of restoration. God's mercy has the power to redeem even the gravest sins when we return to Him with sincerity. May we endeavor to adhere to His teachings, resist temptation, and safeguard the sanctity of marriage.

Reflection Questions:

1. What lessons about obedience and repentance can we learn from David's story?

2. How does coveting lead to greater sins?

3. Why is marriage sacred in God's eyes?

4. How can our actions affect future generations?

5. What does David's restoration teach us about God's mercy?

For Further Study:

Exodus 20:17; Genesis 2:24; Ephesians 5:25–28; Psalm 51:10–17; Proverbs 5:15–23; 1 Corinthians 6:18–20; Exodus 34:7; Deuteronomy 5:18–21; Galatians 6:7–9; Hebrews 13:4.

About The Author

About The Author

Brenda Diann Johnson was born in Dallas, Texas on September 14, 1970 to Robert Johnson and Thelma Byrd. She is the oldest of five children. She has a brother, sister, and two half brothers.

Brenda received her education from the Dallas and Wharton, Texas school systems. She graduated from Government, Law, and Law Enforcement Magnet High School in Dallas. She also received her Bachelor of Arts degree in Communications (Broadcast News) from UTA in Arlington, Texas and her Masters of Education Degree from Strayer University. She has her Texas license in Life, Health, Accident & HMO insurance, her Texas Adjusters License in All Lines, and she is a Texas Notary Public.

Today, Brenda is the CEO/Founder of The Young Scholar's Book Club and ASWIFTT ENTERPRISES, LLC. She is also an experienced educator who has taught and tutored Pre-K through College. Brenda is the Dean of Education, Curriculum & Instruction for Best Practices Training Institute (B.P.T.I). She has also authored books and articles.

From 2001 to 2002, Brenda served as the chairperson for an entrepreneur group called STEP (Sowing Toward Everlasting Prosperity) and as a Center Leader for the Plan Fund.

She also served as the Co-Founder of ASWIFTT Writer's Guild from 2010 to 2019.

In the community, she has served as a volunteer to organizations that help AIDS, HIV, and Syphilis patients.

Brenda currently lives in Texas with her family.

Books and Services
ASWIFTT ENTERPRISES, LLC

Business advertising for Print & Media
BOOK PUBLISHING
RADIO
T.V.
Newspaper

We have affordable advertising packages in our media categories. Some Ads are as low as $35.00. Email to ask about our Business Ads and Commercials.

You can visit us online or e-mail us:
www.aswifttbooks.com
aswifttbookpublishing@yahoo.com

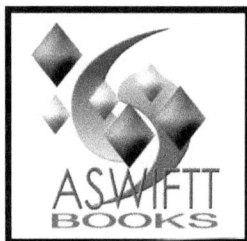

ASWIFTT BOOKS

(Ambassadors Sent With Information For This Time)

ASWIFTT ENTERPRISES, LLC creates businesses that write and publish in all three (3) media genres such as radio, tv, and newspaper that focus on delivering timely, newsworthy and accurate news stories. The media genres also report on local, regional, national and international topics.

The Young Scholar's Workbook:
Book I Vol. I (www.tysbookclub.com)

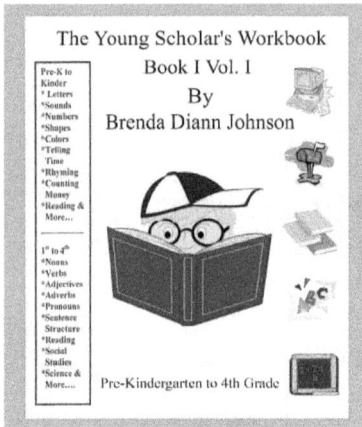

The Young Scholar's
Workbook: Book I Vol. I

By Brenda Diann Johnson

This is a fundraiser
publication for The Young
Scholar's Book Club. 50%
of the proceeds go to help
keep mentoring and tutoring
services free to students.
$19.95 plus s/h

How Did I Get Into This Mess?
You Compromised, Saith the Lord
2nd Edition

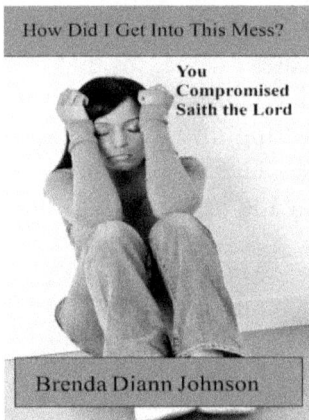

How Did I Get Into
This Mess? You
Compromised, Saith
the Lord 2nd Edition by

Brenda Diann Johnson

$12.95 plus s/h

Articles for Personal Growth and Development: Volume I

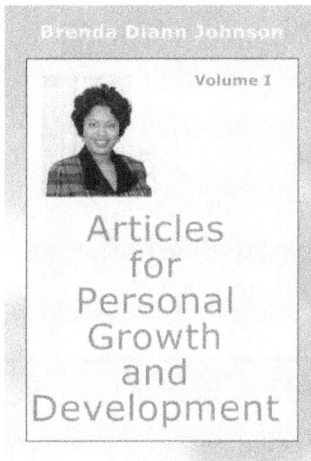

Articles for Personal Growth and Development: Vol. I by

Brenda Diann Johnson

$9.95 plus s/h

My Baby Sister

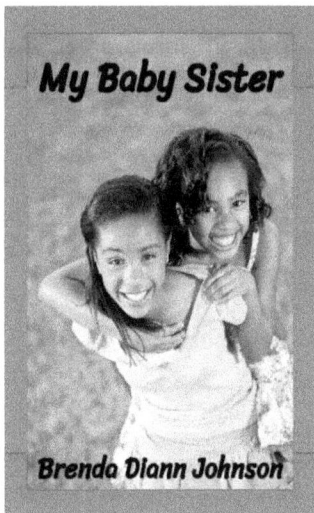

My Baby Sister by

Brenda Diann Johnson

$15.95 plus s/h

Available in English and Spanish

Advertise in

ASWIFTT BOOKS

Your business will have a permanent advertising
spot in an ASWIFTT Book. The book that carries
your Business Ad will continue to advertise your
business every time the book is printed and
purchased by a customer. For more information on
ASWIFTT ENTERPRISES book advertising email
us at: aswifttbookpublishing@yahoo.com

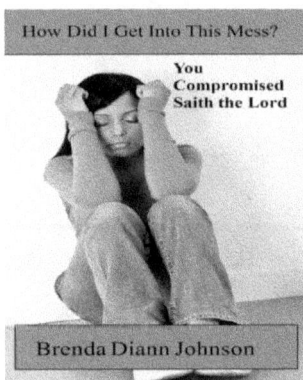

ASWIFTT ENTERPRISES, LLC ORDER FORM

Name_____

Address_____

City_____

State_____

Zip_____
Item _____Amount_____
Item _____Amount_____
Item _____Amount_____

Add $8.50 for Shipping and Handling on books
Total:_____

Make Checks, Money Orders, Cashier's Checks out to:

ASWIFTT ENTERPRISES, LLC

P.O. Box 380669

Duncanville, Texas 75138

Credit Card Orders:
Circle One: Master Card   Visa   American Express
Discover
Credit Card Number_____
Exp. Date_____
Three Digit Security Number on back of
Card_____

Name & Address Associated with Credit Card:

Authorization Signature_____**Date**_____

Your order will be processed or shipped 2 to 4 weeks
from the date order is received. Direct concerns on
orders email: aswifttbookpublishing@yahoo.com
You can also order online at: www.aswifttbooks.com

Thank you for your business! Make copies of this form.

www.ingramcontent.com/pod-product-compliance
Lightning Source LLC
LaVergne TN
LVHW021547080426
835509LV00019B/2893